Another Tuesday at Popcorn Elementary: I

WELCOME TO POPCORN ELEMENTARY!!

Meeka Wojo

COPYRIGHT 2018
MEEKA WOJO
ALL RIGHTS RESERVED

Another Tuesday at Popcorn Elementary: NO BULLIES

DEDICATION

This book is dedicated to everyone who wants a nicer world. Be the Unicorn! –Queen Meeka Wojo

Meeka Wojo

POPCORN ELEMENTARY

MYLIE THE SHEEP

WOLFIE THE WOLF

OTIS THE PIG

DOTTIE THE ELEPHANT

Another Tuesday at Popcorn Elementary: NO BULLIES

AND NOW, THE ADVENTURE BEGINS...

Once upon a time, there lived a fuzzy little pink pig named Otis. He was seven years old and went to Popcorn Elementary School. Every day, Otis the pig packed his lunch and walked to school with Mylie, the purple sheep. They both really loved their school because they get popcorn in class every single day!

Today is a bright and sunny Tuesday morning.

"Bye Mumma!!" exclaimed Otis as he dashed out the door to walk to school.

Another Tuesday at Popcorn Elementary: NO BULLIES

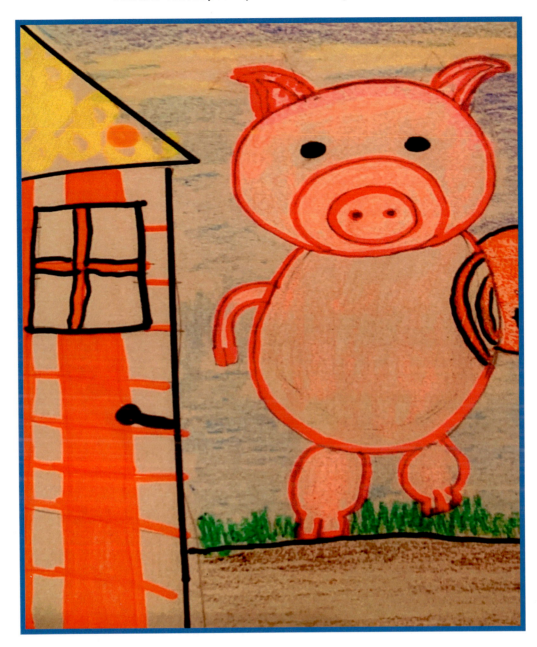

Pounding on Mylie's door, Otis hollered,

"Time for School, Mylie! Come walk with me."

Holding hands, Mylie and Otis began skipping down the sidewalk. Otis asked Mylie a question.

"Why are there not many jokes about popcorn?"

Mylie answers, "I not sure, why?"

In a singing voice, Otis responds, "Because they are corny!" Giggling, they continue on to school.

Meeka Wojo

OUT JUMPED WOLFIE THE WOLF!!!!

"RAAAAAAAAAARRRRRRRRRRRRRRRRRR!"

Another Tuesday at Popcorn Elementary: NO BULLIES

Mylie fell down on the sidewalk. **BOOM!** Rushing, Otis helped her up.

In her sweet little voice, Mylie sobbed.

"I scared ah Wolfie. Wolfie all da time scare me. Every day he scare me."

Another Tuesday at Popcorn Elementary: NO BULLIES

Looking down, Otis noticed her soft purple fur was wet.

"Hum, that mean Wolfie made my friend pee-pee her fur!!!" he thought to himself. As Otis started to gain courage up to tell Wolfie to back off, Wolfie snatched Otis's lunch!!

Wolfie sprinted off laughing.

"Ha ha ha haa haaa! You peed your FUR!"

Otis helped Mylie calm down. Off they went to school. They noticed Dottie the elephant standing on the corner. Dottie saw what happened. Dottie actually saw what happened EVERY morning. She remained silent.

Meeka Wojo

Another Tuesday at Popcorn Elementary: NO BULLIES

When Otis and Mylie got to school, Otis walked Mylie to the nurse's office to get cleaned up. Nurse Kennedy, the teddy bear, asked Mylie, "What did the baby corn say to the momma corn?"

Mylie answered, "I know this one!! Where is POP corn? Ha ha! Like MOM and POP, POPcorn!"

Nurse Kennedy and Mylie smiled. Once cleaned up, Mylie went to her Kindergarten class. Mylie's smile quickly faded. She started picking fur off her hands and looking downward. Mylie was very scared of Wolfie. She silently wished Otis was not in first grade already so they could eat lunch together. The morning seemed to drag on slowly. Watching the clock, Mylie listened for Otis's lunch bell to ring.

Ring! Ring! Ring! The first grade lunch bell rang. Otis sat alone and with just a napkin in front of him. Dottie watched from her table and saw Otis alone and hungry.

"**Again,**" thought Dottie. But, Dottie did nothing but stare.

"Poor piggie," thought Dottie. Other students at her table were pointing at Otis and laughing. Dottie remained quiet, afraid Wolfie or the other students would be mean to her if she spoke up. Mr. Purdue was one of the teachers on lunch duty. Mr. Purdue, a very tall monkey, was juggling bananas then noticed Otis alone.

Mr. Purdue asked Otis, "Would you like to move to a different table?" Otis started crying. Otis told Mr. Purdue about being scared of Wolfie. Otis also told Mr. Purdue what Wolfie repeatedly does to Mylie, and that Wolfie takes his lunch often. Mr. Purdue got Wolfie from his lunch table and walked Wolfie and Otis to the office. They stopped to pick Mylie up from her classroom. Mr. Purdue tried a joke to cheer Otis up.

Another Tuesday at Popcorn Elementary: NO BULLIES

"What music gets popcorn to dance? Hip POP!!" Chuckling alone, Mr. Purdue arrived at the office with the students.

The principal, Mr. Crown Cares, is a tiny kitty that loves tacos. He has a saying he likes.

"Hi students and teachers. Did you know that TACO CAT spells TACOCAT backwards?" Mr. Cares liked to say.

Mr. Cares welcomed them as they entered the office and listened to the whole story. He then asked the students a question.

"Do you know what bullying is?"

Mylie answers, "Mr. Kitty, I mean Kitty Man. Ummm…ummm bullying is a cow dat goes Moo!?" Mr. Cares smiled.

"That is a really great guess! You are thinking of the animal called a bull, Mylie. A bull is different than a **bully.** So, Mylie, my name is actually Mr. Crown Cares. Here at Popcorn Elementary, we do not accept bullying at all. In fact, a fun and easy way to remember what Popcorn Elementary teaches about bullying is to just think of my last name, like this:

CROWN CARES is my name. If you take each letter of my last name, you can think of our anti-bullying program easily. Cares is spelled c-a-r-e-s.

C stands for CREATING.

A stands for, well, just A!

R stands for RESPECTFUL.

E stands for ENVIRONMENT IN...

S stands for SCHOOLS.

Creating a respectful environment in schools. Otis spoke up, "Mr. Cares, excuse me Sir, I never tell on Wolfie, but he steals my lunch nearly **every day.** I was afraid that I would be **tattling** if I told on him. Is that bad?"

Mr. Crown Cares spoke to the students.

"What Wolfie was doing to scare you is called **BULLYING. BULLYING IS INTENTIONAL WHICH MEANS HARMING YOU ON PURPOSE.**"

Mylie squeaked in her little voice, "Yes, Mr. Crown Cares. And and dat Wolfie, he do dat **EVERY SINGLE DAY** to me."

Mr. Cares answered her. "**BULLYING IS REPETITIVE, MEANING IT HAPPENS OVER AND OVER AGAIN.**"

Another Tuesday at Popcorn Elementary: NO BULLIES

    Mr. Purdue listened well. Then he shot his handful of banana peels into the principal's trash can, the students' eyes all popped open big because they were impressed with his basketball skills.

    Mr. Purdue said, "Kids, **tattling** is telling on someone because you want them to get in trouble, and no one is really in danger. Tattling is a situation that does not need an adult's help. **Reporting to an adult is different than tattling**.

You should report something that is a big issue that needs adult attention. Reporting to an adult is kind. If you see someone being bullied and you just let it happen and stay silent, you are showing you agree with the bully's behavior. Sometimes the student being bullied is called **the target**. If you see bullying, REPORT TO A TRUSTED ADULT. Reporting keeps others safe. If it is important and needs adult help, **YOU REPORT IT. REPORTING IS NOT TATTLING."**

Mr. Cares looked at Wolfie in a disappointed way.

"Wolfie, you have made some poor choices. **Since you are trying to SCARE and HARM Mylie and Otis ON PURPOSE and EVERY DAY, that is called BULLYING. BULLYING IS NEVER OKAY."**

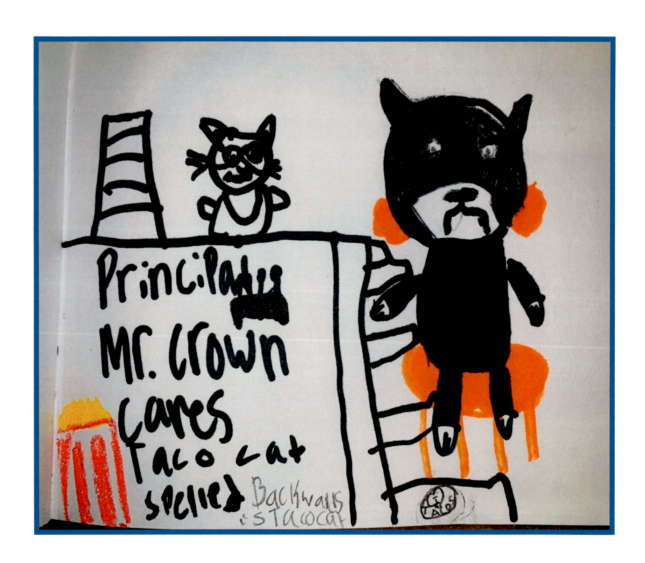

Another Tuesday at Popcorn Elementary: NO BULLIES

BULLYING IS INTENTIONAL

ON PURPOSE

BULLYING IS REPETITIVE

IT HAPPENS MORE THAN ONCE

A BULLY USUALLY HAS POWER

OVER SOMEONE ELSE TO SCARE THEM ON PURPOSE.

The Principal then continued to tell the group, "A bully also can tell lies about you and make fun of you. That is called **gossiping and spreading rumors**.

SAYING, DOING, OR PLANNING TO DO MEAN THINGS IS

BULLYING

AND

BULLYING IS <u>NEVER</u> OKAY!

Mean words and actions are NOT necessary. We all need to keep kindness in our hearts. **BE KIND.** Now students, I want you to remember bullying includes:

THREATS planning to do something mean.

RUMORS AND GOSSIPING telling lies about others or talking about them in a mean way.

HURTING SOMEONE hurting their body or the things that belong to them.

LEAVING SOMEONE OUT on purpose which is called excluding."

The students all looked like they understood and nodded yes. Mr. Purdue smiled and asked Otis, Mylie and Wolfie a question.

"Anyone want to hear a popcorn joke?? …Nah! It is too corny!"

Wolfie looked sad.

"I am sorry Mylie. I am sorry Otis. I will not scare you and steal your lunch anymore. Now I understand what bullying is. I really am sorry and I actually do not know how to make friends. I am so lonely. I thought hurting your feelings would make you pay attention to me. I am SO sorry, Mylie and Otis. Will you please forgive me? Please be my friends."

Mylie and Otis showed their kindness by forgiving Wolfie. Mylie, Otis and Wolfie even started a group called the Bully Patrol. The friends get to visit schools and teach others about bullying using the Crown Cares way of remembering. The students all yelled:

NO BULLIES!

NO BULLIES!

YAY YAY YAY!

NO BULLIES NO BULIES YAAAAAY!

WE LOVE POPCORN WE LOVE POPCORN YAY!!

CROWN CARES AND WE CARE!

Another Tuesday at Popcorn Elementary: NO BULLIES

CROWN CARES: CREATING A RESPECTFUL ENVIRONMENT IN SCHOOLS

THE END

Meeka Wojo

FRIENDSHIP IS HAPPINESS

Another Tuesday at Popcorn Elementary: NO BULLIES

ABOUT THE AUTHOR AND ILLUSTRATOR

My name is Meeka. I am seven years old. As USA National Miss Indiana Princess 2018, I was given the title of Ambassador for Deb Landry's Crown Cares program. She allowed me to base my anti-bullying book on her program for Creating a Respectful Environment in Schools.

I love to volunteer. My hope is to spread kindness and empathy (to understand and share the feelings of another person) to everyone every day. I support many causes, including the Live Out Loud Charity for suicide prevention by Sherrie Gearheart, and Olivia's Cause for alopecia awareness by Sandy Rusk.

Celebrate the individual. Stop the bullying. Save lives. You are strong. You are enough. You are important. I believe in you.

Thank you for reading.

Photo by Kelly Downton Photography

ABOUT THE ILLUSTRATOR

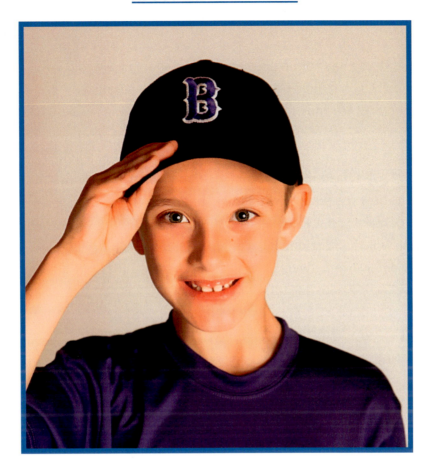

My name is Ivan. I am nine years old. I love sports and I plan to be an astronaut and bring my Mom to space with me.

Photo by Kelly Downton Photography

Meeka Wojo

DISCUSSION POINTS

1. What should Dottie have done differently? (She should have told an adult or spoke up)
2. Where can bullying happen? (Anywhere, including electronics)
3. Name some places we know of that you have seen bullying happen. (On the playground, bus, recess, hallway, lunch, anywhere)
4. Raise your hand for response. How many students have been bullied? Been a bully? Seen a bully? Ask someone who raised their hand what they did when they saw bullying. Ask someone how the felt and what they can do next time.
5. What type of bullying have you seen? (Physical like hitting, kicking shoving. Verbal – saying mean words. Intimidation- scaring or threatening someone.)
6. What is the difference between tattling and reporting? (Reporting is keeping someone safe and tattling is just to get someone in trouble.)
7. WHAT CAN YOU DO IF YOU SEE BULLYING?
   - WALK AWAY AND TAKE FRIENDS WITH YOU
   - CHANGE THE TOPIC
   - INVITE THE TARGET TO JOIN YOU AND YOUR FRIENDS
   - STAND UP TO THE BULLY AND TEL THEM TO STOP
   - GO GET HELP FROM A TRUSTED ADULT

REMEMBER THAT IF IT FEELS BAD OR NOT NORMAL

IT PROBABLY IS!!!

REPORT TO AN ADULT!

Another Tuesday at Popcorn Elementary: NO BULLIES

FRIENDSHIP IS HAPPINESS

What do you call the best student at Corn University?

The A-corn!

Another Tuesday at Popcorn Elementary: NO BULLIES

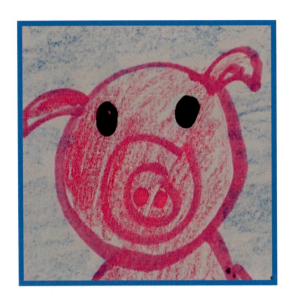

KNOCK KNOCK

WHO'S THERE?

PAPA

PAPA WHO?

PAPAPAPAPAPAPAPAPAPAPAPAPAPAPAPAP POPCORN!

Meeka Wojo

Want to hear another popcorn joke?

Nah, it's too corny.

Bu-byeeee Popcorn People. Booyah!

Another Tuesday at Popcorn Elementary: NO BULLIES

For help, the Live Out Loud Charity for suicide prevention refers to the following:

If you are feeling suicidal, depressed, having relationship troubles, need a sponsor, or someone to talk to please call. If you or someone you know are in an emergency situation please call 911 (if you are USA or Canada based).

Suicide Prevention
USA BASED – OPEN TO INTERNATIONAL CALLERS
1.800.273.TALK
1.800.273.8255

CRISIS INTERVENTION TEXT LINE
741741

Open to all ages, 24/7: Suicidal Thoughts, Self-harm, Depression, Stress/Anxiety, Grief, Eating Disorders, Physical Abuse, Emotional Abuse, Sexual Abuse, Isolation/Loneliness, Relationship Issues, and Bullying.

Depression Hotline USA only
(630) 482-9696

To give to Live Out Loud Charity Directly:

Mail checks payable to Live Out Loud Charity:
Live Out Loud Charity
524 W. Stephenson St., Ste. 209
Freeport, IL 61032

http://liveoutloudcharity.org/about/mission/

To give to Crown Cares Anti-bullying Charity: Mail checks payable to Crossroads Youth Center:

Crossroads Youth Center
199 New County Road
Saco, ME 04072

https://www.crowncares.org/

Meeka Wojo

SUICIDE PREVENTION LIFELINE

1-800-273-8255

1-800-273-TALK

Made in the USA
Columbia, SC
01 March 2019